Dear Parent:

Congratulations! Your child is taking the first steps on an exciting journey. The destination? Independent reading!

STEP INTO READING® will help your child get there. The program offers books at five levels that accompany children from their first attempts at reading to reading success. Each step includes fun stories, fiction and nonfiction, and colorful art. There are also Step into Reading Sticker Books, Step into Reading Math Readers, Step into Reading Write-In Readers, Step into Reading Phonics Readers, and Step into Reading Phonics First Steps! Boxed Sets—a complete literacy program with something to interest every child.

Learning to Read, Step by Step!

Ready to Read   Preschool–Kindergarten
• big type and easy words • rhyme and rhythm • picture clues
For children who know the alphabet and are eager to begin reading.

Reading with Help   Preschool–Grade 1
• basic vocabulary • short sentences • simple stories
For children who recognize familiar words and sound out new words with help.

Reading on Your Own   Grades 1–3
• engaging characters • easy-to-follow plots • popular topics
For children who are ready to read on their own.

Reading Paragraphs   Grades 2–3
• challenging vocabulary • short paragraphs • exciting stories
For newly independent readers who read simple sentences with confidence.

Ready for Chapters   Grades 2–4
• chapters • longer paragraphs • full-color art
For children who want to take the plunge into chapter books but still like colorful pictures.

STEP INTO READING® is designed to give every child a successful reading experience. The grade levels are only guides. Children can progress through the steps at their own speed, developing confidence in their reading, no matter what their grade.

Remember, a lifetime love of reading starts with a single step!

*To Colonel (and cousin) David Snell, who gets to fly all
the time and loves every minute of it.*
—S.E.G.

*To my nieces and nephews—I hope you all get to ride
in a helicopter one day.*
—M.J.D.

Acknowledgments: So many "helicopter people" helped us—on the ground and in the air. Thanks to all those who arranged or participated in photo shoots, including Major Robert Bullock and Lt. Col. James MacDougall of the New York Air National Guard, Scott Palmer of Life Star in Hartford, Connecticut, and Steve Sampson and Eric Sawyer of the Connecticut State Police, and thanks to James Dahill, Steve Brown, and Rob Brigham of Firefly, Inc., for the breathtaking tour of Massachusetts. Several companies were also very generous with their time and photographs— thanks to Rich Zellner, Susan Hitchcock, and Bill Tuttle of Sikorsky; Dennis Hubbard of Erickson Air-Crane; Jenny Jackson, Sally Noyola, and Chris Clegg of Bell Helicopter Textron; and Jim Otto of Hummingbird Helicopters.

Thanks also go to the National Helicopter Museum in Stratford, Connecticut.
Visit www.nationalhelicoptermuseum.org.

And special thanks to Heidi Kilgras, who had a great idea and helped us carry it through.

Photo credits: Cover and pp. 3, 6, 15, 16, 30, 48: Sikorsky Aircraft; pp. 4, 5, 21 (top): Erickson Air-Crane Incorporated; p. 7: Rega Photographic Service; p. 8: © Douglas Peebles/CORBIS; pp. 9, 21 (bottom), 35, 39, 41: AP/Wide World Photos; p. 14: National Air and Space Museum, Smithsonian Institution (SI 93-640); p. 24: Connie Dellera, The Bureau of Land Management; p. 25: © Annie Griffiths Belt/CORBIS; p. 27: James R. Tourtellotte, U.S. Customs Service; p. 28: PH3 Ryan Jackson, U.S. Navy; p. 29: Staff Sgt. Jeremy T. Lock, U.S. Air Force; p. 31: Photographer's Mate 3rd Class John Sullivan, U.S. Navy; p. 33: U.S. Department of Defense; p. 42: Leo Mason/Getty Images; pp. 44–45: © Tom Nebbia/CORBIS.

www.stepintoreading.com

Educators and librarians, for a variety of teaching tools, visit us at
www.randomhouse.com/teachers

Library of Congress Cataloging-in-Publication Data
Goodman, Susan E., 1952–
Choppers! / by Susan E. Goodman ; photos by Michael J. Doolittle. — 1st ed.
p. cm. — (Step into reading. Step 4 book)
ISBN 0-375-82517-7 (trade) — ISBN 0-375-92517-1 (lib. bdg.)
1. Helicopters—Juvenile literature. [1. Helicopters.] I. Doolittle, Michael J., ill. II. Title. III. Series.
TL716.2.G66 2004 629.133'352—dc22 2003026838

Printed in the United States of America First Edition 10 9 8 7 6 5 4 3 2 1

STEP INTO READING, RANDOM HOUSE, and the Random House colophon are registered trademarks of Random House, Inc.

CHOPPERS!

By Susan E. Goodman

Photographs taken and selected by
Michael J. Doolittle

Random House 🏠 New York

Chapter 1

Those Amazing Machines

A forest fire is blazing. The flames are spreading faster than a man can run.

Firefighters chop down trees. They dig trenches. They race to get the fire under control.

A helicopter also helps battle the blaze. It swoops down to a nearby pond. In seconds, it sucks up enough water to fill

50 bathtubs. Then it dumps the water on the fire.

The helicopter starts back to fill its tank again. Then a call comes in. Flames are surrounding some of the firefighters. Soon they will be trapped!

The chopper flies right over. It hovers near the men. Its blades produce a strong wind. The wind pushes the flames back. The firefighters run to safety.

Whirlybirds, choppers, eggbeaters. Whatever you call them, helicopters are amazing machines. Airplanes must move forward to fly. But helicopters can fly forward, backward, and sideways. They can also hover—fly in one spot—as long as they have fuel.

Airplanes need long runways to take off and land. Helicopters can shoot straight up into the air. They can come straight down again.

Helicopters can land in small spaces. They can land on mountains. Some can even land on water. Choppers can go places that cars and planes cannot reach.

Some helicopters zoom along at up to 250 miles an hour. Some fly over three miles high. Choppers can do jobs that other machines cannot.

Scientists who study volcanoes use helicopters all the time. How else could they safely watch an erupting crater and see its lava up close?

During the sixties and seventies, space capsules returning to earth landed in the ocean. A ship was always waiting nearby. But it couldn't get to the astronauts very fast.

The chopper on the ship's deck could. It rushed to find the capsule bobbing in the water. Its job was to carry the capsule back to the ship.

But first, divers jumped out of the helicopter and into the ocean. They swam to the capsule. They opened its door and welcomed the astronauts home.

Here are the basic parts of a helicopter:

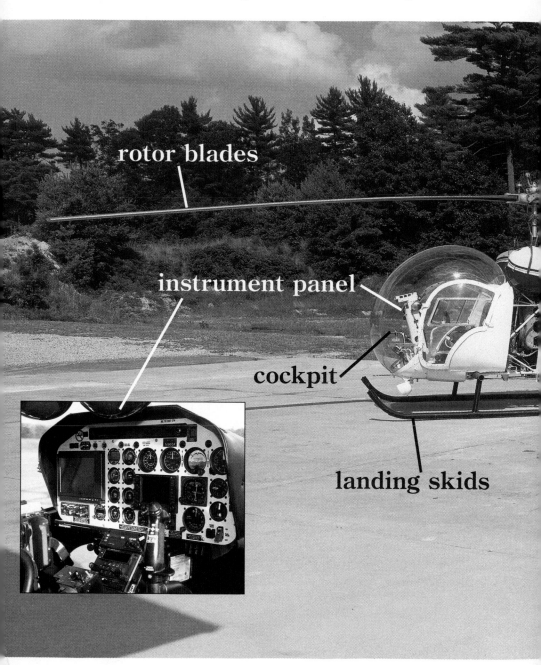

rotor blades

instrument panel

cockpit

landing skids

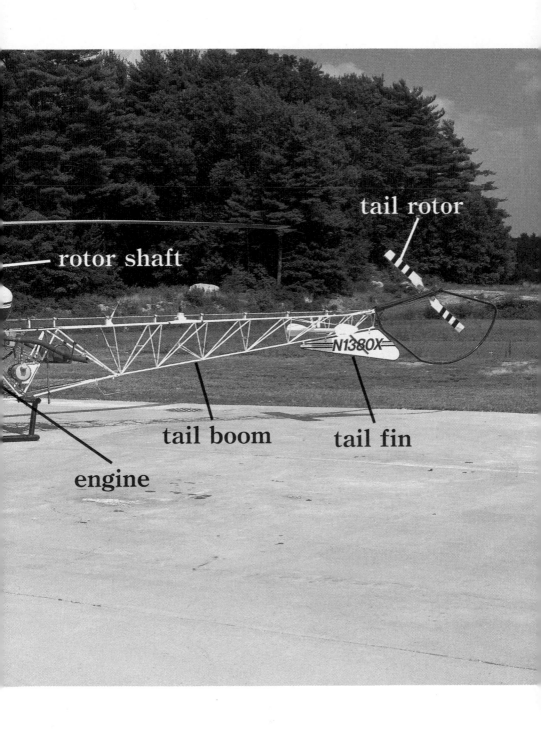

tail rotor

rotor shaft

N1380X

tail boom

tail fin

engine

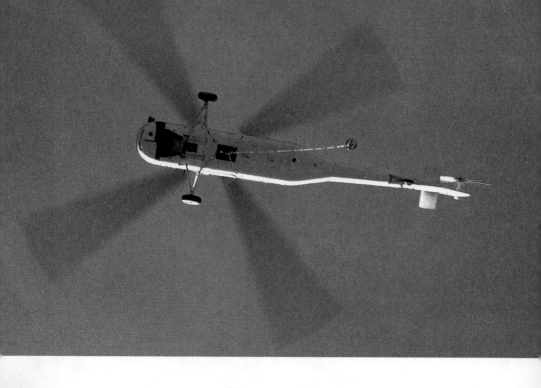

Chapter 2

How Does It Work?

Helicopter blades (or rotors) are actually thin wings. They are shaped like airplane wings.

Air moves past these blades when they spin. The air rushes really fast over the top of the blades. It moves more slowly underneath them. This difference pushes the helicopter into the sky.

A chopper pilot tilts the blades to change direction. To fly forward, the pilot tips them forward. To fly backward, the pilot tilts them back.

Even long ago, people dreamed of using spinning wings to fly. Over 2,400 years ago, the Chinese made flying toys. They worked like this one.

In 1483, the artist Leonardo da Vinci drew his idea of a flying machine. He never built it. (It wouldn't have worked anyway!)

To make a helicopter fly, the blades must turn very fast. They need a light, powerful engine to do the work. The gasoline engine was invented in 1885. With this the helicopter was on its way.

Cornu's early helicopter.

In 1907, a Frenchman named Paul Cornu made the first helicopter flight. His machine only flew for a few seconds. It barely got off the ground. But it was a great start!

As engines got better, so did helicopters. Igor Sikorsky flew the first working American helicopter in 1939. He had added a rotor to the tail. This second set of blades kept the helicopter steady.

In 1945, Sikorsky added another part
to his helicopter—a special hoist. It was a
cable that could be lowered and cranked
up. It could be used to rescue people. This
invention was tested sooner than anyone
could have imagined.

In November of that year, the police
called the helicopter factory. A barge had
crashed into a reef. A hurricane kept other
boats from saving the two sailors on the
wrecked ship.

The Sikorsky helicopter flew to the barge. Its hoist hadn't really been used before.

This test was an important one. It could save two lives.

The pilot lowered the cable. One sailor looped it under his arms. Then up he went.

The helicopter was too small to bring him inside. First he, then his friend, rode through hurricane winds safely to shore.

Chapter 3

Choppers at Work

Not long ago, a family went on a picnic. One minute, the youngest son was there, eating a sandwich. The next minute, he was missing. His parents searched for him for hours. Then they called for help.

Soon the police arrived in their chopper, *Trooper One*. They started flying over the nearby woods. They could not see through the trees. But they didn't need to. The helicopter had a special camera that recorded heat.

Trooper One flew back and forth. Then its pilot yelled out. The camera found a warm object. It was the boy. He was lost in the forest.

Mission accomplished!

Every day helicopters are used to find people, fight fires, and spray crops with chemicals to help them grow. Over land and sea, choppers are hard at work.

Helicopters also help build everything from bridges to buildings to electrical towers. They can even give workers a safe place to stand!

Helicopters can carry very heavy loads. They can also carry people. Choppers called medevacs are flying ambulances. They rush people to hospitals at over 150 miles an hour. And they don't need sirens!

Some helicopters work as "air taxis." They fly into the middle of cities. They can land on top of buildings. Their passengers avoid traffic jams on busy highways.

Other helicopters help the drivers on the roads avoid traffic jams. Radio and television reporters fly high above city streets and bridges. They tell drivers which roads are too crowded to use.

Choppers work in open spaces as well as crowded ones. Out west, wild mustangs run free on the plains. Every few years these horses need a checkup. It used to take cowboys on horseback a long time to find them all. Helicopter "cowboys" round up the horses in no time.

Scientists sometimes catch animals to study them. But getting close to a grizzly bear can be dangerous. So scientists track them with helicopters. From inside the chopper, they shoot the grizzly with a dart. The dart contains medicine to make the bear sleep. Then the scientists can land and do their tests before the bear wakes up.

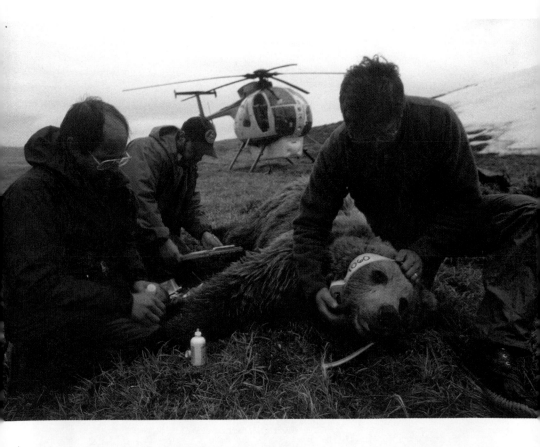

Helicopters can also track criminals. Looking down from the sky, police can search big areas very quickly. They often can find crooks more easily than police on the ground.

A few years ago, some smugglers snuck into the United States to sell drugs. They left by boat. They thought they had gotten away with their crime.

But no! A government chopper was on their trail.

The smugglers' boat was fast. But the chopper stayed right over them. Its engine roared. Its blades created 100-mile-per-hour winds.

The crooks had no way to escape this huge machine. The chopper could follow every move they made. It was time to give up.

Chapter 4

Choppers Go to War

The helicopter is a good soldier for the
military. It does many jobs that trucks and
ships used to do.

In the navy, ships work together in
a group. Smaller boats used to carry
supplies from one big ship to another.

Sailors had to haul the crates on board. It was hard work. Today choppers just drop the loads on the deck.

Trucks still transport troops. But sometimes soldiers fight in places without roads. A chopper can take them there.

Ships and airplanes fire missiles. But they are often far from their target.

Helicopters can also launch missiles toward targets miles and miles away. But they can fly much closer to them, too. Choppers can aim at objects as small as a tank or a car.

And hit them.

Sometimes, however, the *chopper* becomes a target. Enemies aim heat-seeking missiles at it. These missiles chase something hot, like the helicopter's engine. To save the chopper, its pilot shoots off flares. These hot lights can fool a missile into going after them instead.

Choppers perform other jobs during battles. They fly in and spy on the enemy. They protect soldiers with their guns. They help rescue soldiers in trouble.

That's what happened in Iraq in April 2003. Enemy troops were coming toward seven U.S. marines. They had no way to escape.

The marines radioed for help. They waited. Some of them prayed.

First they heard the rumble of rotors. Then they heard gunfire. Their rescue helicopter was flying in low. Iraqi soldiers were trying to shoot it down.

The chopper landed as the Iraqis were closing in. There was no time to lose. The marines leaped inside. Within seconds, the helicopter was on its way.

That time every soldier came back alive.

Chapter 5

Choppers to the Rescue!

One day it began to rain. It rained and rained on the country of Austria. It was the worst storm in 100 years.

One river was like a bathtub with a clogged drain. It overflowed its banks. The river water flooded into a nearby town.

First the water flowed into people's doorways. Then it streamed into windows. But it did not stop there. The water kept rising.

People climbed onto their roofs. Where could they go next?

Into a rescue helicopter!

Choppers can fly almost anywhere to save people. They hover over floods. They zoom into battle.

Sometimes the chopper can't land. Then it drops a cable or a basket. That way, it can lift someone off a roof or out of the water.

Many times rescue workers called parajumpers are there to help. They drop to the ground on ropes. Then they climb back into the chopper—often while carrying someone. Parajumpers must train very hard to learn their job.

Rescue workers save people from mountaintops. They pull people from plane crashes. They help people all over the world.

Once they helped save some fishermen near China. Their ship was far from the shore. Flames were shooting out of its engine room. Soon the boat would sink.

Some men had already jumped into the sea. But a huge storm was coming. The wind howled. Giant waves rolled across the water. Being in the sea was as dangerous as being on the boat.

The helicopter crew threw life jackets to the fishermen. Then they lowered cables. They pulled up two men at a time. They raced to save everyone before the boat went down.

Humans aren't the only ones who get rescued. Once a horse named Caesar fell off a cliff. He dropped 100 feet.

Caesar's legs were cut. So was his cheek. But Caesar was alive.

Caesar was also in trouble. He could not climb back up the cliff. The way down was just as steep.

A vet climbed up to the horse and put bandages on Caesar's legs. Firefighters climbed up, too. They put a sling on Caesar's body. Then they hooked the sling to a helicopter's cable.

Soon Caesar was on his way home.

"Moving a horse wasn't any different from moving other things," said the pilot.

Then he smiled.

"Maybe a *little* different," he said. "People don't cheer when I put a load of concrete down safe and sound."

Chapter 6

Flying for Fun

Choppers work hard so we can play. "Sky limos" take brides to weddings. They carry high school seniors to their proms.

They also take skiers to the top of the world. Helicopters fly to slopes high above roads and lodges. Then skiers race down mountainsides covered with fresh snow. Their chopper is waiting at the bottom, ready to take them up for another run.

A helicopter is also perfect for sightseeing. Want a bird's-eye view of a lighthouse? No problem!

How about a trip to Mount Rushmore? In a chopper, the passengers can look President Lincoln right in the eye!

Moviemakers use the chopper's sky-high view to shoot films. A camera is attached to the helicopter. Sometimes it hangs off the chopper's nose. Then the helicopter flies high and low to film the action.

Helicopters appear in movies, too. They swoop in to help with a daring rescue. They save the star at the very last minute. Sometimes they seem to be the film's real hero.

Seeing a chopper zoom across a movie screen is fun. But pilots say that the best thing about helicopters is being behind the controls.

Learning to fly a chopper begins before you leave the ground. You must know how to use its radio. You must learn to use maps while in the air.

Students must practice flying for a total of at least 40 hours before taking the pilot's test. Most people need even more time to get ready.

Flying a chopper is hard. You must learn to do many things at once. Pilots use both arms and both legs to work the chopper's controls. They say that it's like patting your head and rubbing your tummy—while standing on a beach ball!

They also say that it's worth every second of training.

"It's total freedom," says one pilot. "You move the controls and the helicopter goes wherever you want."

"It's magic," says another pilot. "You're flying up there with the birds!"